DEINONYCHUS

by Janet Riehecky
illustrated by Llyn Hunter

THE CHILD'S WORLD

MANKATO, MN

*Grateful appreciation is expressed to
Bret S. Beall, Research Consultant,
Field Museum of Natural History, Chicago,
Illinois, who reviewed this book to
insure its accuracy.*

Library of Congress Cataloging in Publication Data

Riehecky, Janet, 1953-
    Deinonychus / by Janet Riehecky ; illustrated by Llyn Hunter ;
created by the Child's World.
        p. cm. — (Dinosaur books)
    Summary: Presents knowledge and theory about the physical
appearance and behavior of the dinosaur Deinonychus.
    ISBN 0-89565-625-6 (lib. bdg.)
    1. Deinonychus—Juvenile literature.   [1. Deinonychus.
2. Dinosaurs.]   I. Hunter, Llyn, ill.   II. Child's World (Firm)
III. Title.   IV. Series: Riehecky, Janet, 1953-   Dinosaur
books.
QE862.S3R534   1990
567.9'7—dc20   90-2327
                                                                CIP
                                                                AC

1 2 3 4 5 6 7 8 9 10 11 12 R 98 97 96 95 94 93 92 91

DEINONYCHUS

Some people think that the world of the dinosaurs was a terrible place. After all, the word dinosaur means "terrible lizard."

Most of the time, though, it was a calm
and peaceful world. A dinosaur could relax
and nibble a few tender leaves.

It could, unless, of course, a volcano
erupted with fire and hot rock or . . .

a flood came and swept the whole herd
away.

Sometimes the ground would shake in a
terrible earthquake . . .

or there'd be an unexpected danger, such
as a sudden drop-off.

These were some of the terrors of the dinosaurs' world, but only some of them. Ranking right up there with earthquake, fire, and flood was little Deinonychus (DYE-NON-i-kuss), a dinosaur smaller than many people. It didn't look like much of a threat. It had no armor and no horns. But it had a claw on each back foot that could rip an enemy to pieces. In fact, the name Deinonychus means "terrible claw." Scientists think the Deinonychus was a fast, clever, and deadly hunter—one of the terrors of its world.

very stiff, long tail

Deinonychus stood only four or five feet tall and was about ten feet long. It weighed less than two hundred pounds. That wasn't very big for a dinosaur, but what the Deinonychus lacked in size, it made up for in meanness!

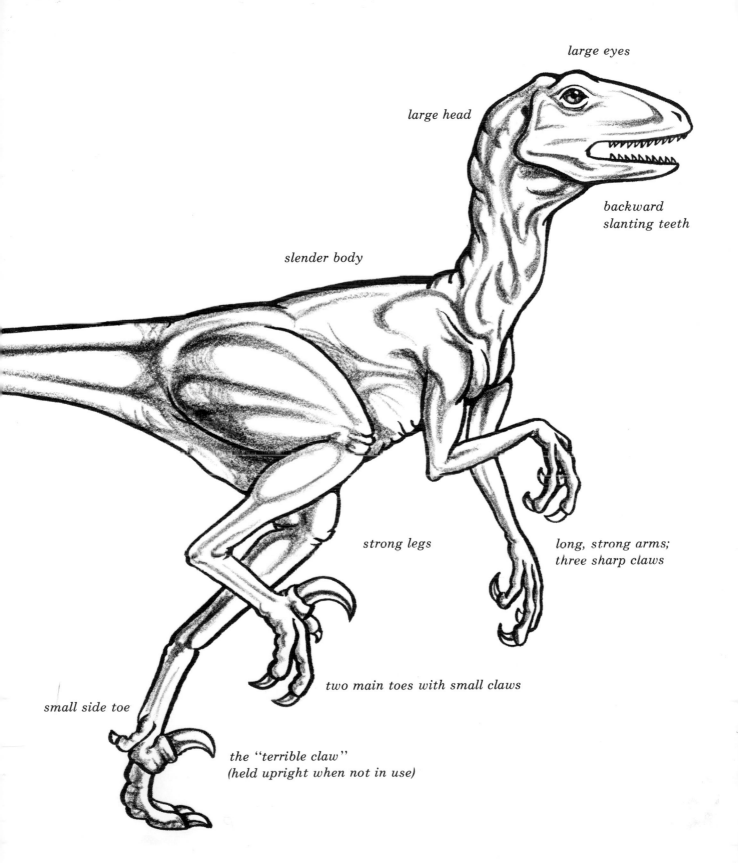

large eyes

large head

backward
slanting teeth

slender body

strong legs

long, strong arms;
three sharp claws

two main toes with small claws

small side toe

the "terrible claw"
(held upright when not in use)

13

The head of the Deinonychus was large, with powerful jaws. It had more than seventy long, sharp teeth. The teeth slanted backwards in its mouth. When its jaws clamped down on its victim, the backward slanting teeth made it almost impossible for the victim to pull away.

But it was the claws on its back feet that really made the Deinonychus terrible. All of the Deinonychus' claws were sharp and dangerous, but the claw on its second toe was deadly. It was five inches long and razor-sharp.

As it walked, the Deinonychus balanced on just two toes, holding its special claws up off the ground. The Deinonychus didn't want those weapons to drag on the ground and get dull.

If a Deinonychus saw a small, tasty-looking dinosaur, it gave chase. Deinonychus was a fast runner and could outrun just about any other dinosaur. When it ran, it held its tail out stiffly behind for balance. It could also swing the tail to one side or the other to help it swerve right or left quickly and easily.

When the Deinonychus caught its prey,
it grabbed hold of it with the sharp claws
on its hands (front feet). Then it balanced
on one back foot and—slash! slash! Down
came the terrible claw to kill the victim.

As if that weren't terrible enough, scientists think the Deinonychus also hunted in packs. A pack of Deinonychus could defeat just about any other kind of dinosaur.

Armored dinosaurs were pretty safe from most meat-eaters, but not from Deinonychus. Some scientists think a pack of Deinonychus would attack a small armored dinosaur. The pack would charge in and flip the armored dinosaur over on its back. An armored dinosaur was as helpless as a turtle rolled onto its back. The pack could finish it off easily. Only an armored dinosaur too heavy to flip was truly safe.

Probably the favorite prey of a pack of Deinonychus was the one-ton dinosaur, Tenontosaurus (ten-ON-tuh-sawr-us). The Tenontosaurus was a strong dinosaur, and it grew to a size ten times that of a Deinonychus. But the pack didn't let size alone bother it—that just meant a bigger dinner!

Scientists think a pack of Deinonychus would hide, waiting for a Tenontosaurus to stray from its herd. Large eyes and sharp senses made the Deinonychus very good at seeing without being seen. When a Tenontosaurus came close, the pack would leap to the ambush.

First the pack would chase the Tenontosaurus, trying to leap onto its back. They needed to take it by surprise or wound it quickly to slow it down, because the Tenontosaurus was one of the few dinosaurs that could run faster than the Deinonychus. If the pack managed to leap onto the Tenontosaurus' back, they'd hold fast with the claws on their hands and slash with the terrible claws on their feet.

Tenontosaurus would fight back.
Sometimes it would strike with its stiff.
heavy tail. Sometimes it would roll over
and try to crush the creatures clinging to
its back. It might kill a few Deinonychus.
But it is unlikely that it would defeat the

entire pack. The Deinonychus were quick, and most could probably jump free before the Tenontosaurus could roll over on top of them. Then they only had to wait until the wounded Tenontosaurus weakened and fell. Dinnertime!

The Deinonychus may have liked fighting so much that they even fought each other. Some scientists think the males fought one another to see who would be the leader of the pack or to decide who got to live in the best area. They don't think the dinosaurs fought to the death, but that they probably had quite some fights.

Possibly the only thing that wasn't terrible about the Deinonychus was the way
it raised its babies. Scientists think it was
smart enough to take good care of its little
ones. It probably fed them and protected
them while they were young . . .

and then taught them to hunt when they
got older.

The Deinonychus was one of the fiercest dinosaurs ever to live. It proved that "terrible" things can come in small packages.

Dinosaur Fun

One of the most exciting things about dinosaurs is that we still have lots to learn about them. Scientists continue to make discoveries that often change our old ideas and tell us more about how dinosaurs lived. And who knows how many "new" dinosaurs will be discovered in the future?

To keep on top of the latest dinosaur discoveries, look through newspapers and magazines for articles about and pictures of dinosaurs. Ask your parents to help you. Clip the articles and keep them in a dinosaur scrapbook. How many articles do you think you will find in one month? In one year? You may even need to start a second scrapbook!